ENFP: MY BRAIN IS AN IDEA FACTORY

Insights into Your Emotions, Relationships, and Career

Asa Eccleston Kibilski

CONTENTS

WELCOME TO YOUR IDEA FACTORY: UNDERSTANDING THE ENFP MIND

Your alarm jolts you out of a dream so vivid you're half convinced it was real: You were riding a unicorn across a rainbow, leading a band of woodland creatures in a musical revolution, and simultaneously designing an eco-friendly amusement park. As you open your eyes, the remnants of the dream linger, and a question pops into your head: "Should I try to make that unicorn thing happen?" Before you can settle on an answer, a new thought bursts in: "I should start a blog! No, a podcast! Wait, maybe an online course about... how to make your dreams a reality?!"

Welcome, fellow ENFP, to the wondrous, whirlwind world of your mind. It's a place where ideas flow like waterfalls, enthusiasm bubbles like champagne, and possibilities unfurl like infinite petals of a magical flower. If your brain feels like a constant fireworks display, a never-ending symphony of half-formed plans and exhilarating "what if?" scenarios, you've come to the right place.

You, my friend, might just be an ENFP. It stands for Extroverted, Intuitive, Feeling, Perceiving – a personality type within the Myers-Briggs framework. Essentially, it means you're a visionary with a big heart, an unquenchable thirst for connection, and a knack for seeing the extraordinary in the ordinary. You thrive on those "lightbulb" moments, new experiences, and the magic of human interaction.

Let's paint a picture of this ENFP life. You're the person who gets unreasonably excited about discovering a quirky new coffee shop. You're the one who can spark a lively debate about the meaning of life while waiting in line at the post office. You can turn a simple walk in the park into an impromptu photo shoot, complete with dramatic poses and philosophical musings about the squirrels. You're the friend everyone calls when they need a burst of optimism, a creative solution, or just a good laugh. Your zest for life is infectious, even if your overflowing calendar is slightly less so.

But being an ENFP isn't always sunshine and butterflies. Underneath all that sparkling energy, there's also a thinker, a feeler, and occasionally, a doubter. Sometimes, your mind races so fast you trip over your own thoughts. You're a natural-born multitasker, but your passion projects outnumber the hours in a day. You crave deep connection, yet the fear of being misunderstood can hold you back. You want to change the world, but the sheer scale of it all can feel overwhelming at times.

This book is your invitation to dive headfirst into the beautiful chaos that is your ENFP self. We'll explore the superpowers of your personality – your boundless enthusiasm, your gift for seeing potential, your unwavering belief in the goodness of people. But we'll also tackle those pesky ENFP challenges – the tendency to overthink, the struggle to focus, the ever-present battle against procrastination.

Think of this as your personal operating manual. We'll uncover strategies to channel those brilliant ideas, navigate your whirlwind emotions, and find ways to recharge your batteries when the world gets a bit too noisy. Most importantly, we'll celebrate the unique and wonderful person you are. Because being an ENFP, with all its exhilarating highs and occasional stumbles, is an extraordinary gift.

Your journey through your brilliant, beautiful, and delightfully unpredictable idea factory is about to begin!

THE SPECTRUM OF ENFP: UNDERSTANDING THE TURBULENT AND ASSERTIVE VARIATIONS

Within the vibrant community of ENFPs, a fascinating spectrum exists. While all ENFPs share those core traits of enthusiasm, idealism, and a knack for connection, there's a crucial distinction that influences their experience of life: the Assertive (-A) and Turbulent (-T) variations. Think of them not as separate personality types, but as two points on a sliding scale, each with unique strengths and challenges.

Turbulent ENFPs: The Sensitive Striver

Turbulent ENFPs encompass those who often experience their rich inner world with a heightened level of intensity. Here's what sets them apart:

- Sensitivity Amplifier: They feel emotions deeply – both the exhilarating joys and the heart-wrenching lows – and external feedback can land with amplified impact.
- The Perfectionist Phantom: Driven by a desire for excellence, Turbulent ENFPs can fall prey to self-doubt and crippling fear of failure, constantly questioning if their work is "good enough".
- Seeking External Validation: They crave recognition and affirmation, which can make them prone to people-pleasing and taking criticism more personally than their Assertive counterparts.
- Rumination Station: Turbulent ENFPs tend to overanalyze social interactions, decisions, and potential missteps, sometimes spiraling into anxiety or self-reproach.

The Turbulent ENFP Superpower: Deeply Attuned & Empathetic

Those sensitivities, while challenging, are also the source of their greatest strengths:

- Empathy Supernova: They have an uncanny ability to intuit the emotions of others, making them incredibly supportive friends, advocates, and healers.
- Passion with Purpose: Their sensitivity fuels a deep desire to create positive change and fight for what they believe in.
- Introspective Explorers: Their tendency to overthink drives a thirst for self-understanding and personal growth.
- Artistic Expression: Turbulent ENFPs often channel their emotions into creative outlets, producing beautifully moving and poignant works.

Assertive ENFPs: The Confident Trailblazer

Assertive ENFPs radiate a sense of inner confidence and generally navigate their internal and external worlds with more ease. Here's how they stand out:

- Resilience Boost: They bounce back more readily from setbacks and criticism, viewing them as stepping stones rather than personal indictments.
- "Good Enough" Mantra: More comfortable with imperfection, they're driven by striving for excellence rather than an unattainable ideal.
- Inner Compass: Assertive ENFPs trust their intuition and are less swayed by the opinions of others, making decisions based on their values.
- Go-Getters: They possess a self-assuredness that propels them to pursue their dreams, taking calculated risks with less fear holding them back.

The Assertive ENFP Superpower: Unwavering Optimism & Action

Their confidence unlocks unique strengths:

- Infectious Enthusiasm: They exude a positivity that inspires and motivates those around them, naturally drawing people into their orbit.
- Changemakers: Assertive ENFPs see possibilities and take bold steps towards making their visions a reality.
- Less Prone to Burnout: Their resilience helps manage the emotional rollercoaster, reducing the likelihood of withdrawing in exhaustion.
- Cheerleading Squad: They champion others' potential, lifting up those around them with genuine support.

The Spectrum of Self-Growth

Here's the key takeaway: Neither Turbulent nor Assertive is inherently better. Both possess incredible strengths, and both face unique challenges. Understanding where you fall on this spectrum empowers you with the self-awareness to:

- Turbulent Growth: Focus on building resilience, taming the inner critic, and celebrating progress over perfection.
- Assertive Growth: Be mindful of potential blindspots, practice vulnerability, and focus on deepening connections beyond the surface-level.

This chapter is about celebrating the diversity within the ENFP type. It's about recognizing your unique tendencies, learning strategies tailored to your needs, and channeling your energy in ways that maximize your potential for joy and meaningful contribution. Whether you're a Turbulent or Assertive ENFP (or somewhere in between!), embrace the journey of becoming the most authentic and fulfilled version of yourself.

THE JOY OF BEING EXTRA: EMBRACING YOUR ENTHUSIASM

Picture this: You're at a party, and the music is just starting to pump. Suddenly, an irrepressible urge to dance overtakes you. It's not just a gentle sway or a polite head bob – you're talking full-on interpretive dance moves with a side of impromptu karaoke. The rest of the room might give you sidelong glances or amused smiles, but you're in your element. The rhythm, the energy, the sheer joy of movement – it's infectious. Before long, a few others join in, and soon enough the whole place is buzzing.

That, my fellow ENFPs, is the power of your enthusiasm. It's not just a feeling; it's a force of nature, a radiant beam of sunshine bursting through the clouds of the mundane. It's what makes you the life of the party, the friend who can turn a rainy Tuesday into an adventure, the person who inspires others to see the world in a brighter, more vibrant light.

But sometimes, even for us ENFPs, that boundless enthusiasm can feel a bit...well, a lot. Maybe you've been told to "tone it down" or worried about coming across as too intense. Maybe you secretly fear your exuberance makes you seem scattered or even a little bit naive. But here's the thing: your enthusiasm is a superpower, not a flaw. It's what makes you uniquely you, and it's time to embrace it wholeheartedly.

Let's talk about why your enthusiasm is so darn awesome:

- Contagious Joy: Think of your enthusiasm as glitter. It gets everywhere, in the best possible way. When you're genuinely excited, it sparks something in others. It reminds them of the simple joys, the possibilities just waiting to be discovered.
- The Antidote to Cynicism: In a world that often feels

heavy and jaded, your enthusiasm is a refreshing breeze. You inspire hope, reminding people there's still magic to be found, even in the most unlikely places.

- Fuel for Creativity: Enthusiasm is the spark that ignites your ideas. It's the boundless energy that pushes you to try new things, think outside the box, and find unique solutions to life's challenges.
- Magnet for Connection: People are drawn to genuine enthusiasm. It makes you approachable, magnetic, and the kind of person others want to be around. Your joy creates space for others to express their own.

Of course, like any superpower, there's potential for the occasional mishap. You might jump headfirst into a project, only to have your enthusiasm fizzle halfway through. Sometimes you overshare, bursting with so much to say that it can leave others feeling a little steamrolled. But don't worry; we'll address those challenges too.

The key is learning to channel your enthusiasm, to use it as fuel, not a runaway train. This chapter is all about embracing that joyful energy, understanding how it serves you, and discovering ways to harness it for maximum awesome – without accidentally setting anything on fire (metaphorically speaking, of course).

So, grab your dancing shoes and a megaphone (kidding…sort of), and let's dive into the exhilarating world of ENFP enthusiasm!

SUPERPOWER OR KRYPTONITE?: EXPLORING ENFP CREATIVITY

If your idea of a perfect evening involves brainstorming a business plan with your best friend, transforming your living room into a canvas splatter zone during a spontaneous painting session, and scribbling the first draft of a novel before bed – you, my friend, are channeling your inner ENFP creativity. It's a force that seeps into every aspect of your life, from your fashion choices to the way you solve problems.

Think of your creativity as a bubbling cauldron of possibilities, constantly simmering with new ideas, connections, and unconventional perspectives. You don't just see the world as it is; you see the world as it *could* be. A cardboard box isn't just for storing old sweaters; it's a potential spaceship, a puppet theater, or the foundation for an elaborate fort. A boring meeting isn't just a waste of time; it's an opportunity to brainstorm ways to revolutionize the company's workflow (or at least doodle some seriously impressive cartoon characters in the margins).

Let's break down why your creativity is one of your greatest strengths:

- The Idea Generator: Your mind is a constant whirlwind of possibilities. You see connections others miss, turning the ordinary into the extraordinary. When faced with a challenge, you don't just search for a solution; you generate a dozen solutions... and a few more, just for fun.
- Natural Innovator: You're not content to follow the status quo. You're driven to explore, experiment, and find better ways to do things. You're the one who suggests a wacky team-building exercise, reimagines the office layout, or invents a new cocktail using leftover ingredients.

- Problem Solver Extraordinaire: Thanks to your out-of-the-box thinking, you have a knack for finding creative solutions to even the stickiest of problems. Stuck in a traffic jam? You turn it into an impromptu dance party. Project falling apart? You rally the team with a hilariously absurd brainstorming session.

- The Artist Within: Whether you express yourself through painting, music, writing, or building LEGO masterpieces, your creativity finds outlets in unexpected ways. It's not just about the final product; it's about the process, the joy of self-expression, and transforming raw ideas into something tangible.

However, like a powerful potion, ENFP creativity needs to be handled with care. Sometimes it explodes in glorious technicolor; other times, it fizzles out just as quickly as it appeared. Here's where those ENFP kryptonite moments might creep in:

- Idea Overload: Your mind races with so many possibilities that it can be crippling. You start projects with unbridled enthusiasm, only to get overwhelmed and abandon them halfway through.

- Fear of Imperfection: The sheer number of ideas also breeds a fear of choosing the "wrong" one. You worry that your creations will never be good enough, leading to procrastination or creative paralysis.

- The Distractible Artist: Shiny new ideas are like squirrels darting across the road– irresistibly distracting! You can switch focus in a heartbeat, sometimes leaving unfinished projects in your wake.

- Misunderstood Genius: Your big leaps and unconventional thinking aren't always appreciated by those who prefer a more practical approach. You might hear feedback like "that's unrealistic" or "focus on one thing at a time."

But fear not, my fellow creative warriors! This chapter is about harnessing your wild and wonderful creative energy.

Think of it as a treasure hunt within your own mind. The rewards – a sense of fulfillment, the thrill of seeing your ideas come to life, and the simple joy of creative expression – are well worth the adventure. Let's get started!

WHEN INTUITION IS YOUR COMPASS: TRUSTING YOUR GUT

ENFPs have a secret weapon, a sort of sixth sense that guides them through life: intuition. It's that inner voice, the sudden flash of insight, the "aha!" moment that seems to come from nowhere and everywhere at the same time. Unlike cold, hard logic, intuition is a messy, magical, and surprisingly powerful force. It's what allows you to see beyond the surface, connect seemingly unrelated dots, and make decisions that might baffle those around you, but feel absolutely right within your own soul.

Think of those moments when you just *knew* something was going to happen. Maybe you had a hunch about a new job opportunity that appeared out of the blue and it turned out to be a perfect fit. Or perhaps you sensed tension in a friendship before any words were spoken, allowing you to address the issue with sensitivity. These are your intuitive powers at work!

But here's the thing about intuition: it's often subtle, fleeting, and easily drowned out by the noise of the world. It whispers while logic shouts. ENFPs, with their love of exploring options and possibilities, can sometimes find it challenging to trust those inner nudges, especially when they contradict external advice or what seems like 'common sense'. So, let's explore why your intuition is a precious gift and how to hone this innate superpower:

- The Inner Compass: Intuition provides a sense of direction when the path ahead is unclear. It's that feeling in your gut guiding you towards choices in alignment with your values, even when the outcome is uncertain.
- Spotting the Unsaid: ENFPs are naturally perceptive, picking up on subtle cues, unspoken emotions, and hidden

motivations. Your intuition helps you read between the lines and understand what really drives both yourself and others.

- The Human Connection: Intuition fuels your ability to build deep, meaningful relationships. It allows you to 'feel' the energy of a room, empathize with others, and anticipate their needs, making you a friend who just gets it.
- The Spark of Creativity: Those sudden flashes of inspiration, the way seemingly unrelated ideas come together? That's your intuition at play. It allows you to think outside the box and generate innovative solutions others might miss entirely.

Of course, intuition isn't infallible. Sometimes you might misinterpret a gut feeling because of your own biases or emotional state. Here's how to know when and how to trust those inner whispers:

- Getting Quiet: Intuition speaks loudest when you take moments of stillness. Meditation, mindful walks, or simply journaling can create space for your inner compass to recalibrate.
- Know Your Triggers: Are you prone to anxiety or easily swayed by others? Recognize the factors that cloud your intuition and develop practices to get back to a neutral place.
- Gut Check vs. Wishful Thinking: Be honest with yourself. Is that flash of insight a true hunch or merely hoping for a desired outcome?
- Data + Intuition = Genius: Balance those inner knowings with research and input where possible. Intuition isn't about making reckless decisions, but guiding wise ones.

This chapter is about learning to trust your unique inner voice. We'll delve into exercises to sharpen that intuitive sense, distinguish genuine gut feelings from wishful thinking, and find ways to confidently navigate life's decisions – big and small – with your inner compass as a guide.

THE STRUGGLE IS REAL: OVERTHINKING, PROCRASTINATION, & OTHER ENFP WOES

Welcome to the not-so-secret side of the ENFP personality – the place where overthinking dragons lurk, procrastination gremlins wreak havoc, and your brilliant ideas sometimes get lost in the labyrinth of your own mind. Don't worry, you're not alone! These are classic ENFP struggles, born from the same strengths that make you so awesome. So, let's shine a light on these shadowy corners and find ways to conquer those inner demons.

Overthinking: The Endless Loop

You know those moments when a simple question turns into an existential crisis? You analyze every angle, envision every worst-case scenario, and create a spiderweb of "what ifs" so complex it would make a conspiracy theorist jealous. An innocent comment from a friend spirals into a relentless internal monologue: "Did I say something wrong? Are they secretly mad at me? Maybe I should just move to a deserted island and become a hermit..."

Why it happens: Your curious mind and big-picture thinking are incredible gifts, but they can trip you up. You spot possibilities others miss, which, unfortunately, includes potential pitfalls and hidden snags. Your empathy makes you acutely aware of others' feelings, leading you to overanalyze every interaction.

The Downside: Overthinking drains your energy, paralyzes your decision-making, and fuels anxiety. It can also lead to taking things too personally or reading into situations that have nothing to do with you.

Procrastination: The Great Delay

Your calendar is a chaotic masterpiece – jam-packed with exciting projects, inspiring workshops, and social plans. But when the time comes to start one of those tasks...whoosh! You vanish like a ninja, reappearing only after successfully reorganizing your sock drawer, binge-watching an obscure documentary, and attempting to teach your cat to yodel.

Why it happens: It's not laziness; it's often a mix of factors. Excitement leads you to pile on new ideas before finishing existing ones. Perfectionism makes starting seem daunting. And let's face it, sometimes the admin side of brilliant ideas is just plain boring.

The Downside: Procrastination leaves promising projects unfinished, creates unnecessary stress, and can damage your reputation as the one who's always brimming with plans but rarely follows through.

The Rest of the Crew

There are a few other ENFP troublemakers worth mentioning:

- Distractibility: Your mind is a butterfly, flitting from idea to idea. A text notification, a bird singing outside your window, an itch on your left foot – anything can divert your focus.
- Impulsivity: When enthusiasm strikes, it's tempting to jump in headfirst without considering the practicalities. This can lead to overcommitting, rash decisions, or accidental promises you later regret.
- People Pleasing: Your heart craves harmony and makes you deeply attuned to others' needs. But this can lead to prioritizing others' happiness over your own well-being and bending yourself into a pretzel to avoid disappointing someone.

Taming Those Inner Beasts

Fear not! These pesky ENFP tendencies don't have to define you. This chapter is all about equipping you with tools and tactics to slay those dragons and unleash your brilliance with less self-sabotage along the way. We'll cover:

- Breaking the Overthinking Loop: How to quiet that mental chatter, challenge negative assumptions, and separate legitimate concerns from anxiety-fueled spirals.
- Befriending Procrastination: Strategies to beat procrastination by breaking down tasks, battling perfectionism, and making exciting ideas less intimidating.
- Embracing the Power of Focus: Tips to manage distractions, prioritize projects, and channel that amazing laser-focus you definitely possess when the situation calls for it.
- Saying No (Kindly but Firmly): How to set healthy boundaries, prioritize your time, and protect your energy without feeling perpetual guilt.

Consider this chapter your personal demon-slaying boot camp. By understanding where these challenges stem from, you gain power over them. Get ready to reclaim your time, energy, and those brilliant ideas that deserve to see the light of day!

FINDING YOUR PEOPLE: THE POWER OF AUTHENTIC CONNECTION

Imagine this: You walk into a room full of strangers and within minutes, you've found yourself engaged in a deep conversation, sharing stories, and laughing as if you've known each other for years. You leave that room feeling energized, understood, and maybe even a little inspired. That, my ENFP friend, is the magic of finding your people.

For ENFPs, connection is more than just socializing; it's essential fuel for your soul. You crave deep bonds, authentic conversations, and the feeling of being seen and appreciated for your unique self – quirks and all. Finding people who genuinely "get" your whirlwind mind, appreciate your enthusiastic tangents, and celebrate your big-hearted dreams is an essential ingredient to living a joyful and fulfilling life.

So, why do those "right" connections matter so much? Let's dive in:

- Your Energy Source: When you connect with like-minded souls, their excitement fuels your own. They recharge those ENFP batteries with support, encouragement, and just the right dose of chaotic fun.
- Feeling Understood: Being an ENFP can sometimes feel a bit like being an alien who speaks a language only vaguely resembling Earthling-speak. Finding people who get your humor, appreciate your long-winded theories, and won't judge your midnight dance-party-for-one makes a world of difference. It validates your unique way of being in the world.
- Growth Fuel: Your tribe challenges you in the best way. They push you outside your comfort zone, offer new perspectives, and help you see the blind spots your optimism sometimes

obscures.

- The Cheerleading Section: ENFPs have big dreams and need people rooting for them. Your tribe celebrates your wins, lifts you up through setbacks, and reminds you of your strength when self-doubt creeps in.
- Making an Impact: Amplify your ENFP desire to change the world for the better by finding people who share your values and causes. You inspire each other and make a bigger positive ripple effect together.

Spotting Your Kindred Spirits

But here's the thing: Not all connections are created equal. So, how do you find those genuine, life-affirming friendships? Look for these qualities:

- Shared Values: Find people whose core beliefs align with yours, whether it's a passion for social justice, a love for silly puns, or a commitment to personal growth.
- Appreciation for Your Quirks & Depth: True connection goes beyond surface-level charm. Your people should love your goofy sense of humor while also engaging with your deepest thoughts.
- Mutual Investment: Look for friends who are as willing to listen as they are to share, investing equally in the relationship's growth.
- Unconditional Support: You need people who will cheer you loudest when you succeed and be there to offer a soft place to land when you stumble.

Building Your Connection Toolkit

Finding those special connections takes effort, especially in a world that sometimes values small talk over big ideas. Here's your ENFP connection toolkit:

- Vulnerability is Your Key: Being your open, genuine self is the fastest way to draw in people who resonate with you.
- Follow Your Interests: Join clubs, volunteer for causes, or

attend niche events. Passion is where you'll find potential soulmates.

- Quality Over Quantity: It's not about having hundreds of acquaintances; a few deep connections are worth their weight in gold.
- Nurture Existing Bonds: Appreciate the friends you have! Be present, invest in those relationships, and make space for them in your busy ENFP life.

LOVE, ENFP STYLE: FROM BUTTERFLIES TO SOULMATES

Think of ENFP love like a kaleidoscope – ever-changing, vibrant, and filled with dazzling patterns that shift beautifully with the slightest tilt. It's falling headfirst, heart bursting with a million fluttering butterflies. It's deep midnight conversations, passionate debates, and unwavering support for each other's wild and wonderful dreams. And even on those less-than-sparkly days, it's ultimately about choosing that person, not just the giddy feeling, but the messy, complex, gloriously real whole of who they are.

ENFPs in Love: Your Superpowers

You bring a unique kind of magic to relationships. Here's what makes your approach to love so special:

- The Sparklighter: ENFPs create an atmosphere of warmth, fun, and possibility. You see the best in your partner, inspiring them to reach their full potential, even when they don't believe in themselves.
- The Deep Diver: You crave connection that goes beyond surface level. You want to know your partner's soul – their fears, their dreams, the weird song lyric they've had stuck in their head since childhood.
- Communication Virtuoso: Whether it's heartfelt declarations of love or playful teasing, you express yourself with authenticity and flair. You're also a natural empathizer, making your partner feel truly heard and understood.
- Master of Adventure: Everyday routines? Those make ENFPs break out in hives. You transform even mundane outings into mini-adventures, keeping things fresh and exciting. You remind your partner that life is meant to be explored, hand-in-hand.

Of Course, There's a Flipside

Love, even for us ENFPs, isn't always sunshine and rainbows (though we certainly prefer the rainbows!). Here are those classic ENFP blind spots that need mindful navigation:

- The Idealist's Curse: Your love of possibilities makes you prone to falling for the potential of a person rather than who they truly are. Infatuation can make you overlook red flags or idealize someone who isn't quite soulmate material.
- Need for Space vs. Fear of Abandonment: You crave freedom to explore your interests and recharge those creative batteries. But this can be misunderstood as emotional distance, leaving your partner feeling neglected or clingy.
- Conflict Avoidance: Your people-pleasing instincts can lead you to ignore problems rather than risk tension. But unresolved issues fester, eroding even the strongest connection.
- Intensity + Sensitivity = Fireworks: You feel emotions deeply, both the exhilarating highs and the hurt-so-bad lows. This can lead to passionate outbursts one day and wounded withdrawals the next, leaving your partner bewildered.

Soulmate Seekers: Your Quest for the One

ENFPs yearn for that deep soulmate connection, someone who sees the world through a similar mix of idealism, wonder, and a sprinkle of mischievous fun. You want a partner-in-crime, a cheerleader for your crazy schemes, and a soft place to land when the world feels a bit too harsh.

So, how do you distinguish true love from the fleeting crush? Here's your compass:

- It's a Two-Way Street: They see and appreciate *your* unique brand of awesome, flaws and all. It's not just about them being swept off their feet by your charisma.
- Growth Fuel: This relationship challenges you in healthy

ways, pushing you to step outside your comfort zone and become a better version of yourself.

- Ease + Effort: True love has a beautiful rhythm. There's comfort and ease alongside the willingness to work through the messy stuff.
- Team Players: You both celebrate individual passions and support each other's dreams with genuine enthusiasm. There's no room for jealousy or competition.

ENFPS AT WORK: WHEN PASSION MEETS PURPOSE

Imagine a workplace where big ideas flow freely, brainstorming sessions resemble wild improv shows, and colleagues feel more like a supportive family than coworkers. That, my friends, is the dream scenario for most ENFPs. You thrive in environments that value creativity, collaboration, and a genuine desire to make a positive impact. The traditional 9-to-5 cubicle routine? That's more like your personal version of soul-crushing torture. So, how do you leverage your ENFP superpowers to find work that fuels you instead of draining you? Let's dive in!

Understanding Your Work Needs

Forget about "shoulds" and societal expectations. These are the elements of a fulfilling career for an ENFP:

- Purpose-Driven: You don't just need a paycheck; you need work aligned with your values, making a tangible difference in someone's life, or the world at large.
- Growth Potential: Learning is your fuel. You're turned off by jobs where skills stagnate and every day looks like the last.
- People-Centered: Connection and collaboration aren't just a perk for ENFPs; they're essential for job satisfaction. Sharing ideas, problem-solving together, and building genuine bonds with colleagues is crucial.
- A Splash of Chaos: While rigid routines may strangle you, a bit of organized chaos isn't just tolerable, it's energizing. You thrive in dynamic environments where projects change, deadlines shift, and unexpected opportunities appear.

Workplace Superpowers... and Kryptonite

Your unique strengths make you an incredible asset – if you're in the right environment. Here's what you bring to the table:

- The Spark Plug: Your enthusiasm is infectious, motivating teams and boosting morale. You bring fun and creativity, turning even mundane tasks into something more enjoyable.
- Big-Picture Visionary: You can see the potential impact that a boring spreadsheet can have on changing lives. This perspective helps others connect their day-to-day work with the bigger mission.
- Master Collaborator: ENFPs bring people together, valuing diverse perspectives and facilitating discussions where everyone feels heard.
- Problem-Solving Wizard: With your out-of-the-box thinking and ability to connect seemingly unrelated concepts, you can see solutions that leave everyone else scratching their heads in awe.

Of course, those strengths can flip into challenges in the wrong work setting:

- Easily Understimulated: Routines and repetitive tasks turn your vibrant mind to mush. You need variety, challenge, and new things to learn.
- Scatterbrain Struggles: Your love of exploration can make you jump from task to task too quickly, sometimes jeopardizing deadlines if not managed consciously.
- Allergic to "Just Because": Don't tell an ENFP to do something simply because it's the way it's always been done. You need to understand the purpose to stay motivated.
- Sensitive Soul: Harsh criticism or a negative work environment can bruise an ENFP more than others, making you withdraw or feel a sense of failure quickly.

Finding Your Fit

The quest for that dream job where you feel challenged, energized, and appreciated requires strategy! Here's your action plan:

- Forget Job Titles: Focus on the kind of work,

company culture, and overall mission. Open your mind to unconventional paths or even crafting a unique role.

- Network Like a Pro: Tap into your people skills. Attend events related to fields that excite you, and let your network know what you're searching for. Hidden opportunities often emerge through connections.
- Honest Interviewing: Assess the workplace vibe as much as your potential tasks. Are people enthusiastic? Is collaboration valued? Does it feel supportive?
- Advocate for Yourself: Don't be afraid to ask for the flexibility you need, whether it's opportunities to work on multiple projects or the occasional work-from-home day to recharge.

This chapter is your roadmap to designing a work-life that nourishes your soul. We'll explore career paths that often resonate with ENFPs, break free of the "shoulds", and uncover the hidden gems within your existing role to find greater satisfaction.

THE FINE ART OF SAYING NO: SETTING BOUNDARIES WITHOUT GUILT

Picture this: You're already juggling three projects, two volunteer commitments, and plans to reorganize your sock drawer by color... when another "opportunity" lands on your already overflowing plate. It could be an exciting project, a favor for a friend, or an invitation to that networking event you vaguely remember mentioning sounds interesting. A tiny voice whispers "Take it!", fueled by your enthusiasm for new possibilities. But deep down, you know saying yes means sacrificing sleep, sanity, or disappointing others down the line.

This, my fellow ENFPs, is the eternal struggle of the people-pleaser. Your heart is generous, your enthusiasm boundless, and your fear of missing out (FOMO) is a real and powerful force. But learning to say "no" with grace and conviction is essential for protecting your well-being, staying focused on your goals, and building strong, genuine relationships.

Why Saying "No" is So Darn Hard

Here's why even the most confident ENFPs can find "no" a four-letter word:

- Disappointing Others: You genuinely want to help, you crave connection, and you don't like the feeling of letting someone down.
- Fear of Judgement: Part of you worries that saying "no" will make others think you're selfish, lazy, or somehow less worthy.
- Shiny Object Syndrome: New opportunities sound exciting! Saying "yes" initially feels way more fun than missing out.

- Internal Pressure: You hold yourself to high standards and feel the need to do it all, and do it all perfectly.

The Benefits of Mastering "No"

Think of boundaries as protective armor for your energy, focus, and well-being. Here's what you gain by embracing the power of "no":

- Respect and Authenticity: People actually respect you *more* when you're honest about your limits. They'd rather you said "no" upfront than overcommit and underdeliver.
- Deeper Connections: When you prioritize quality over quantity in your relationships, you invest more in the ones that truly matter.
- Focus and Fulfillment: Saying "no" creates space to excel at your chosen priorities and experience true fulfillment, rather than feeling scattered and burnt out.
- Regaining Control: Setting boundaries puts you back in the driver's seat of your life, reminding you of your power to choose.

The Art of the Gentle but Firm "No"

So, how do you actually *say* those two little letters without dissolving into a puddle of guilt? Here's your script:

1. Empathize: Acknowledge the other person's request and that it's coming from a good place. "I appreciate you thinking of me" or "That sounds like an amazing project" shows you're listening.
2. Be Clear and Direct: Don't over-explain or apologize profusely. A simple "I'm not able to take that on right now" is usually enough.
3. Offer Alternatives (Optional): If you genuinely want to help, provide options: "I'm swamped this week, but could I help you next week?" or "Can I recommend someone else who might be a great fit?"

Boundary Bootcamp: Your Training Guide

Here's how you train your "no" muscle:

- Start Small: Practice declining small requests first. Can't do a coffee run? Pass on the extra cookie? Small wins build confidence.
- Tune In: Pay attention to that gut feeling of "oh, no..." when asked to do something. That's an early warning sign to heed.
- Know Your Priorities: What are your non-negotiables? Time with family? Creative projects? Health? Keep these front and center when faced with requests.
- Guilt Reframing: Instead of "I'm letting them down", try "I'm honoring my own needs" or "I'm being a good friend to myself".

This chapter is your permission slip to prioritize *you*. It's about making conscious choices, not knee-jerk reactions driven by people-pleasing instincts. Because let's be real, saying "yes" when you really mean "no" is a disservice to everyone involved – including yourself.

THE ENFP SURVIVAL GUIDE: NAVIGATING A WORLD BUILT FOR OTHERS

Let's be honest – the world isn't exactly designed with ENFPs in mind. Society seems to reward people who are predictable, who color neatly inside the lines, and whose idea of fun is meticulously organizing their spice rack. Meanwhile, you, my fellow enthusiast of chaos, are overflowing with ideas, craving deep connection, and likely have a spice rack that's organized by impulsively purchased whims, not alphabetically. This can lead to feeling misunderstood, undervalued, or like you're constantly trying to fit a gloriously vibrant, multi-dimensional puzzle piece into a very square hole.

But here's the good news: Embracing your ENFP-ness is a superpower, not a liability. And with a few navigational tools and a healthy dose of self-compassion, you can not only survive but thrive in this world that sometimes operates at a different frequency.

Survival Strategy #1: Embrace Your Inner Weirdo

Stop trying to hide your sparkle to blend in with the beige. The world needs more of your quirky jokes, your genuine empathy, and whatever delightfully random project you're currently obsessed with. When you try to suppress those parts of yourself, you dim your own light and exhaust your precious energy. Give yourself permission to be authentically, unapologetically you – whether that's wearing mismatched socks on purpose or breaking out into spontaneous dance moves at the grocery store. It might make others giggle, raise a few eyebrows, but it'll make your soul sing.

Survival Strategy #2: Find Your Recharge Rituals

ENFPs are like high-powered gadgets with amazing capabilities but short battery life. You absorb the energy around you – both the joyful kind and the soul-sucking kind. This means regular recharging is non-negotiable. Discover what truly renews your spirit: solo time immersed in nature? A creative project where you can lose yourself for hours? Mindlessly binging a show with a fuzzy blanket and zero obligations? Schedule these rituals into your life like the most important appointments and guard them fiercely.

Survival Strategy #3: Build Your Focus Muscle

That flitting butterfly mind of yours is a beautiful thing, but it needs occasional guidance. Left unchecked, it can sabotage your best intentions. Here's the deal: ENFPs *can* focus, but it likely won't look like the laser-like precision of some personality types. Experiment with techniques like the Pomodoro method (short bursts of work with breaks), keeping a running "brain dump" list to park distracting ideas, and finding accountability partners to keep you on track.

Survival Strategy #4: The Art of the Strategic "Yes"

You can't do it all, and trying leads to burnout city. Become a connoisseur of the strategic "yes" – the commitments that truly light you up and align with your bigger goals. To do this honestly, you need a crystal clear idea of your top priorities. Is it growing your side hustle? Spending more quality time with loved ones? Whatever it is, use that as your compass when deciding where to invest your precious energy.

Survival Strategy #5: Befriend the J Types

Those organized, practical, plan-loving folks (you know who they are) might seem like your polar opposites. But, they possess strengths that complement your own beautifully. Seek trusted "J" types who can be your sounding board, help you break down big projects into manageable steps, or simply remind you to check if you actually have a dentist appointment that day. Embrace their structure-loving ways for mutual benefit.

This chapter is a reminder that you're not alone in the feeling that the world moves to a different beat sometimes. It's about finding strategies that work *for* you, not trying to force yourself into a mold that was never meant for your glorious, unbridled ENFP spirit. Lean into the things that make you uniquely you, and build a life that supports your quirks, your passions, and your endless desire to make the world a more interesting, and joyful, place.

TAMING THE IDEA TORNADO: FINDING FOCUS AMIDST THE CHAOS

Imagine your mind as a bustling marketplace, overflowing with vendors shouting about their wares, acrobats performing gravity-defying feats, and curious creatures you've never seen before emerging from the crowd. This thrilling spectacle is your ENFP mind at its finest. But sometimes, that bustling marketplace can turn into a chaotic tornado, tossing brilliant ideas, unfinished projects, and random musings into a swirling vortex that makes it difficult to get anything done.

Focus, for an ENFP, isn't about becoming a productivity robot or suppressing your creative energy. It's about harnessing that glorious chaos, giving form to those swirling ideas, and finding the calm within the storm. Think of it like building a beautiful, organized garden out of a wild, untamed jungle – both are magnificent in their own ways, but one is simply easier to navigate and produce those lovely blooms you crave.

Strategy #1: Brain Dump & Conquer

Your mind is a goldmine of ideas, but they need a place to exist outside your head. Get into the habit of regular "brain dumps". Grab a notebook, a giant whiteboard, or your favorite note-taking app and let it all fly out. Bad ideas, brilliant ideas, half-formed thoughts, song lyrics stuck in your head – no judgments! The simple act of externalizing all that mental clutter creates space for clarity. Once it's out, you can sort, categorize, prioritize, and finally act on what deserves your attention.

Strategy #2: One Thing at a Time (Mostly)

Multitasking is an ENFP's superpower and curse. Embrace your ability to juggle multiple projects...strategically. Choose one main task to focus on for a set amount of time (try the Pomodoro technique: 25 minutes on, short breaks in between). Knowing you can bounce to something else later eases the pressure, allowing you to dive deeper into the task at hand. For the truly important tasks, eliminate those shiny distractions. Close those extra browser tabs! Silence your phone, and give yourself the gift of deep focus for even a short burst of time.

Strategy #3: The Excitement Filter

New ideas are like shiny objects to an ENFP – irresistible! Before jumping headfirst into a new project, run it through a quick filter. Is it genuinely exciting and in alignment with your bigger goals? Or is it just a distraction disguised as inspiration? Channel that brilliant curiosity into exploring your existing projects more deeply rather than always adding new ones to the pile.

Strategy #4: Done is Better Than Perfect

Perfectionism is the enemy of progress, especially for ENFPs. The desire to get everything "just right" can paralyze you, leading to unfinished projects and a nagging sense of frustration. Embrace the concept of "good enough". Aim for excellence, but remember that shipping something out into the world, even if it's not 100% flawless, is infinitely better than it collecting dust in the eternally "in progress" corner of your mind.

Strategy #5: Accountability Buddies

ENFPs thrive on connection. Find people who believe in you and gently (but firmly) help keep you on track. This could be a mentor, a friend, or a mastermind group. Share your goals, report on your progress, and let them cheer you on or give you a friendly nudge when you get sidetracked. Knowing someone else is invested in your success is incredibly motivating.

FROM DREAM TO DONE: MAKING YOUR IDEAS A REALITY

ENFPs are the dreamers, the visionaries, the ones who see a world bursting with possibility and potential. Your mind is a kaleidoscope of ideas, each more vivid and exciting than the last. But the true magic of being an ENFP lies not just in the dreaming, but in translating those magnificent visions into reality. This chapter is your step-by-step guide to bridging that gap between "wouldn't it be cool if..." to "I made this happen!"

Step 1: Capture the Magic

Those fleeting moments of inspiration, those bursts of "aha!" – don't let them vanish like smoke. Develop a system to capture every idea, big and small. Carry a notebook everywhere (a fancy leather-bound one or a crumpled napkin, it doesn't matter), utilize voice memos on your phone, or dedicate a wall of your space to sticky notes filled with scribbled dreams. The key is to have a designated "idea catcher" readily available, so inspiration never escapes.

Step 2: Trim the Fat

It's time to separate the truly brilliant from the merely interesting. Review your collection of captured ideas with a critical but kind eye. Ask yourself: Does this align with my bigger goals? Does it fill me with a deep sense of excitement and purpose? Be ruthless about prioritizing the ideas that light a fire within you. Let the others go with a smile, knowing that your time and energy are best spent on what truly matters.

Step 3: Break It Down

Grand visions can feel intimidating. The path from brilliant idea to finished project might seem shrouded in mist. This is where your need for the big picture works in your favor. Take that exciting idea and reverse engineer it. What are the smaller steps, the individual milestones, the tiny actions required to move it from concept to reality? Break it down until each step feels manageable, even the ones that seem a little bit boring.

Step 4: Embrace the Imperfect Start

Don't wait for all the stars to align, the perfect resources to appear, or to feel 100% confident. ENFPs learn by doing. Start messy, start small, but start. Write that first draft, even if it's terrible. Take that initial step towards building your website, even if you're a tech novice. Momentum is your friend, and action breeds clarity.

Step 5: Find Your Implementation Style

ENFPs aren't known for their rigid adherence to plans, but some structure goes a long way. Experiment with different systems that suit your work style. Try time blocking, visual project boards, or collaborate with a detail-oriented friend who can keep you on track. The goal is to find the sweet spot between enough structure to stay focused and enough flexibility to let your creativity flow.

This chapter is your roadmap to turning that beautiful, buzzing idea factory into a tangible reality machine. It's about trusting your vision, even when the path is unclear, and finding joy in the messy, magical process of creation. Now, get out there and make some magic happen! After all, the world needs more of your unique brand of brilliance, not just hidden away in that magnificent ENFP mind of yours.

WHEN PERFECTIONISM ATTACKS: EMBRACING "GOOD ENOUGH"

For ENFPs, the pursuit of perfection is a double-edged sword. Your desire for excellence fuels your creativity and passion for making a difference. You have big visions for yourself, your projects, and for the world. High standards push you to achieve great things. But that perfectionist voice inside your head – the one that insists everything must be flawless before anyone can see it – can be a creativity killer and a major source of self-sabotage.

Picture this: You've spent days, maybe even weeks, working on a project that lights your soul on fire. But when it's time to share it, a wave of fear washes over you. What if it's not good enough? What if people judge my work, or worse, judge *me*? That crippling perfectionism convinces you it's better to keep your creation hidden than risk it being less than perfect. So it sits on your hard drive, in that unfinished sketchbook, or as a half-formed idea inside your head, robbing you and the world of its potential.

Let's dismantle those perfectionist myths that hold you back:

Myth 1: Perfection = Worthiness. Your perfectionist voice links your work's value to your self-worth. It's a trap! Your worth is inherent, regardless of whether your project is a smashing success or a stepping stone on the path to something even greater.

Myth 2: Mistakes = Failure. Perfectionism equates mistakes with personal failure. In reality, mistakes are teachers, feedback in disguise. Embracing imperfection is essential to growth and innovation.

Myth 3: Done Is Better Than Perfect. Your inner critic scoffs at this notion. But waiting for perfection is a recipe for never getting anything out into the world. A project 80% complete that serves others is infinitely more valuable than one collecting digital dust in pursuit of an unattainable ideal.

Embrace the Power of "Good Enough"

"Good enough" isn't about mediocrity, it's about giving yourself grace. Set standards of excellence, then aim for the sweet spot between doing your best work and meeting deadlines or sharing your creations. When that perfectionist voice rears its head, ask yourself: Is this truly critical for the project's success, or is it a fear-fueled attempt at self-protection? Focus on progress, not perfection, and celebrate each step as a victory.

Strategies to Conquer Perfectionism

Here's your toolkit for combating perfectionist paralysis:

- Reframe Feedback: Seek feedback early in the process. This shifts your mindset from fearing criticism on a finished product to seeing it as valuable input to improve your work.
- The 80% Rule: Set a deadline and commit to releasing your project once it reaches 80% of your ideal vision. Those last few tweaks rarely make a significant difference compared to getting it into the hands of those it's meant to serve.
- Celebrate the Imperfect: Find role models who embrace vulnerability and release work that isn't polished to perfection. Their example shows that authenticity often resonates far more than unrealistic standards.

This chapter is about rewiring your brain to celebrate progress, learning from missteps, and finding the freedom to share your gifts with the world, even when they feel a little bit wobbly. Remember, ENFP, done is infinitely better than perfect, because done has the power to change lives, including your own.

THE POWER OF POSITIVE FEEDBACK: FUELING YOUR ENFP ENGINE

ENFPs, with your big hearts and enthusiasm for connecting with others, truly thrive on positive feedback. It's not just about ego-stroking (though a well-timed compliment is always delightful). For you, genuine appreciation and positive reinforcement are like fuel for your creative engine. It validates your ideas, encourages those sometimes-shaky leaps of faith, and reminds you on the tough days that yes, what you bring to the table matters.

But here's the thing: You can't rely solely on external sources for that feel-good energy boost. Learning to champion yourself, to celebrate your own wins, and to cultivate an inner cheerleader as relentlessly optimistic as you are for others is a key skill for a thriving and happy ENFP life.

Why Positive Feedback Matters So Much

- Validation: ENFPs are often brimming with offbeat ideas and unconventional approaches. Positive feedback affirms that you're not just crazy, those sparks of brilliance might be onto something truly amazing.
- Motivation: When you're pouring your heart into a project, appreciation keeps you going, especially during those middle stages where the finish line seems far away.
- Connection: ENFPs crave connection, and positive feedback strengthens your bonds with others. It fosters a sense of collaboration and reminds you that you're not alone in your endeavors.
- Confidence Booster: Let's face it, ENFPs experience self-doubt like everyone else. Positive feedback, both from others and yourself, combats that inner critic and reminds you of

your strengths.

Cultivating Inner Cheerleading

Here's how to become your own biggest fan:

- Wins Jar: Make it physical! Write down accomplishments, big and small, on slips of paper and drop them in. On rough days, pull a few out as reminders of your awesomeness.
- Self-Appreciation Ritual: Schedule time for self-reflection. Acknowledge what you're proud of, what challenges you overcame, and the progress you made, no matter how small.
- Kinder Inner Critic: Replace harsh self-judgment with curiosity and compassion. "Why did that feel difficult?" opens a door for self-understanding that "I suck" slams shut.

Actively Seeking (and Receiving) Feedback

- Be Specific: Instead of "Did you like it?", ask targeted questions: "What worked well in this presentation?" or "What resonated most with you about this project?".
- Source Matters: Choose people whose opinions you genuinely respect and trust. Vague praise from a stranger means less than targeted feedback from a mentor.
- Practice Gratitude: Express sincere thanks for those who take the time to offer feedback, even if it includes constructive criticism.

This chapter is about celebrating what you do well and learning to fuel your own fire. It's about seeking out feedback that nourishes your growth, trusting your instincts, and celebrating your journey with as much enthusiasm as you celebrate the journey of those around you. Because the world needs confident, self-assured ENFPs who believe wholeheartedly in their ability to make a positive impact.

REST & RECHARGE: SELF-CARE FOR THE SCATTERBRAINED

Imagine your ENFP energy as a wildly enthusiastic puppy. Boundless enthusiasm, easily distracted by anything shiny, and adorable...until it pees on the rug because you've been having so much fun playing that you forgot about pesky necessities like bathroom breaks. Self-care is the ENFP equivalent of lovingly teaching that puppy healthy habits for a long, happy, and (mostly) house-trained life.

The Struggle is Real: Why ENFPs Need Conscious Recharge

Your vibrant energy and care for others are superpowers, but they come with a unique Kryptonite: Overstimulation and burnout. Here's why those ENFP batteries drain dangerously fast:

- Empath Extraordinaire: You absorb emotions around you – the good, the bad, and the energetically messy. This can leave you feeling drained, even if you're not consciously aware *why*.
- Novelty Seeker: Your brain craves new experiences, information, and connections. But constant input without processing time leads to mental overload. Ever feel scattered after a whirlwind of activities, even ones you enjoyed? That's your signal.
- FOMO Central: That fear of missing out? It drives you to say "yes" more than healthy, leading to an overpacked schedule and sacrificing downtime your body and mind desperately need.
- People Magnet: Your warmth and energy attract others. While connection fuels you, it's easy to give too much without remembering to replenish your own well.

Redefining Self-Care

Forget about bubble baths and scented candles (unless that's genuinely your jam, then carry on). ENFP self-care is about honoring your unique needs, not following a generic checklist. Here's your action plan:

Identify *Your* Drainers & Delights

What leaves you feeling depleted? Social events? Admin tasks? Sensory overload? Likewise, what truly recharges you? Alone time in nature? Spontaneous dance parties in your living room? Be specific. Your self-care plan needs to address your unique energy patterns.

Recharge Rituals: Schedule them like non-negotiable doctor's appointments. Block out solo time, creative play sessions, or mindless activities (hello, reality TV binge!) that allow your brain to unwind. Consistency is key.

Boundaries 101: Learn to say "no" *before* you hit the wall of exhaustion. Protect your downtime and be selective about social events. It's better to fully show up for a few things than be half-present everywhere.

Embrace Stillness: Even short moments of mindful breathing or meditation calm the overactive ENFP mind. Struggle to sit still? Start small with focused walks in nature or simply noticing sensations in your body.

Permission to Experiment: Your self-care plan will evolve. Don't get stuck in a rigid routine that feels like another chore. If hiking recharged you last week and dancing is what you need today, honor that!

Guilt-Busting Reminders

Here's the truth your inner critic tries to hide:

- Self-care isn't selfish, it's essential. A drained ENFP benefits no one. You radiate more positive energy when fully charged.
- It's about joy, not just duty. Find self-care activities that

spark delight, not just obligation.
- Recharge = Better Connection. Those deep bonds you crave? They're stronger when you have the emotional capacity to be truly present.

OWNING YOUR AWESOMENESS: DITCHING SELF-DOUBT

ENFPs, with your boundless enthusiasm, big dreams, and tendency to see the potential in everyone and everything, can sometimes struggle to see that same extraordinary potential within yourself. Self-doubt, that sneaky little gremlin, plants seeds of uncertainty. "Am I good enough? Do I have what it takes? What if people realize I'm just faking it?" This undercurrent of insecurity can undermine your confidence, prevent you from stepping fully into your power, and sabotage your chances of achieving the amazing things you are destined for.

But here's the secret, oh brilliant ENFPs: That self-doubt isn't the whole truth. It's a warped filter distorting your perception of yourself. It's time to ditch that filter, reclaim your brilliance, and step into the unapologetically awesome person you were always meant to be.

Why ENFPs Are Prone to Self-Doubt

Let's dissect that inner critic:

- The Idealist's Curse: You see the world as it *could* be, which is glorious. But this also magnifies the gap between your current reality and those big dreams. It's easy to feel "not enough" when you're always striving for something more.
- Fear of Judgement: Your deep desire for connection makes you sensitive to how others perceive you. Any hint of criticism can tap into that deep-seated fear of not being liked or not belonging.
- Multipotentialite Woes: Your many interests and talents can lead to "shiny object syndrome", making you doubt your choices and wonder if you should be focusing on a "more practical" path.

- Comparisonitis: Social media is a highlight reel of everyone else's seemingly perfect lives. It's easy to fall into the trap of comparing your behind-the-scenes mess to others' curated feeds, fueling that inner critic's voice.

Your Anti-Doubt Toolkit

Here's how you shift from self-doubt to unwavering self-belief:

- Evidence Journal: Challenge those negative thoughts! For every "I'm not good enough", find proof to the contrary. Past accomplishments, positive feedback, moments where you overcame a challenge – document it all!
- Separate Potential from Perfection: You are not your future accomplishments; you are a work in progress with immense capacity for growth. Focus on the journey of becoming, not an unrealistic standard of flawlessness.
- Inner Compassion: Talk to yourself as you would your best friend. Replace harsh judgment with understanding. Instead of "I always mess this up", try "This feels difficult right now; how can I learn?"
- Embrace the Quirky: Those offbeat passions, your unorthodox thinking? Those are the source of your unique brilliance. Let go of societal "shoulds" and champion what makes you, well, you.
- Progress over Perfection: Celebrate small wins and focus on consistent action, not some magical end state of being "perfect enough".

Own Your Awesomeness: The Exercise

Here's a powerful task to shift your perspective:

1. Your Eulogy: Imagine your future funeral (morbid, yes, but powerful). What do you want people to say about your life? What contributions, qualities, and impact do you want to be known for?
2. Reverse Engineer: Look at those eulogy words. What actions, big and small, can you take TODAY to embody that person?

It might be acts of kindness, finally starting that creative project, or simply prioritizing joyful experiences.

This chapter is about recognizing that self-doubt is merely a habit of thought, not your defining truth. It's about remembering your inherent worthiness, embracing your unique journey, and confidently walking into a future that matches the brilliant, compassionate, and vibrantly awesome person you truly are.

WHEN FEELINGS GET LOUD: UNDERSTANDING ENFP EMOTIONS

ENFPs, your superpower is feeling things deeply. You experience joy with an intensity that makes the whole world seem to sparkle. Empathy flows through you like a river, connecting you to the emotional currents of those around you. You have a natural gift for bringing light to the darkest corners of others' hearts. But that same sensitivity means your own feelings can sometimes hit you like a tidal wave – overwhelming in both their wondrous highs and their gut-wrenching lows.

The ENFP Emotional Landscape

Let's paint a picture of your emotional world:

- Intensity: You don't do lukewarm emotions. Joy can feel like pure euphoria; sadness can pull you into the depths of despair. The volume dial is always set to extra.
- Empathy Overload: You feel others' emotions as if they were your own. This makes you an incredible support system, but can also drown you in the negativity around you.
- Idealism vs. Reality: Your heart yearns for deep connection and a world without suffering. These grand ideals can clash with the messy and hurtful realities of life, leaving you feeling frustrated, angry, or disillusioned.
- Passion = Fuel: Your emotions, whether positive or challenging, fuel your creativity, your determination to make a difference, and your thirst for experiences that stir your soul.
- Sensitivity = Vulnerability: That big, open heart makes you incredibly attuned to subtle cues and unspoken needs. However, it can also leave you sensitive to criticism or

perceived rejection.

Navigating the Emotional Rollercoaster

Here's where things get tricky:

- Bottling It Up: ENFPs are often social chameleons, adapting to the energy of those around them. Stuffing down your own feelings to avoid burdening others can lead to emotional explosions later.
- Seeking External Validation: Your strong desire for connection can make your emotional state dependent on how others are feeling – a recipe for instability.
- Rumination Station: That analytical mind can overthink emotions to a dizzying degree, creating spirals of anxiety or amplifying hurt feelings.
- The Extrovert Hangover: Socializing fuels your fire, but sometimes, the aftermath is a crash landing of emotional exhaustion and the need to retreat entirely.

Emotional Mastery: Your Toolkit

Learning to harness your emotional power is essential to thriving as an ENFP. Here's how:

- Name to Tame: Identify and name your emotions without judgment. Even the messy ones deserve to be witnessed. Simply saying "I feel overwhelmed" or "This wave of anger is scary" lessens their grip.
- Body Awareness: Emotions are felt physically. Learn your body's signals. Tightness in the chest? Stomach churning? Pay attention to what your body is telling you, providing clues to the underlying emotion.
- Mindful Expression: Find healthy outlets for those intense feelings. Journaling, creative expression, movement, or talking it out with a trusted confidant who can simply listen.
- Boundaries, Boundaries, Boundaries: Learn to set limits to protect your emotional well-being. This means saying "no"

to energy vampires and stepping back from situations that consistently leave you drained.

- Celebrate the Joy: Don't just focus on managing the difficult emotions. Savor the good ones! Practice gratitude, express your delight, and intentionally cultivate experiences that spark your unique sense of joy.

This chapter is about honoring the full spectrum of your emotional experience. The goal isn't to become less sensitive, but to build emotional intelligence. Develop tools to ride those powerful waves instead of being swept away by them.

THE GROWTH MINDSET: EMBRACING LEARNING & CHALLENGES

ENFPs, with your boundless curiosity and thirst for new experiences, naturally gravitate towards growth. You're driven by that desire to learn, explore, to become the most amazing, authentic version of yourself. But let's be honest, growth isn't always sunshine and butterflies. It's stumbling blocks, uncomfortable stretching, and confronting those stubborn parts of yourself that resist change.

Developing a true "growth mindset" means embracing the whole messy process – the exhilarating breakthroughs and the frustrating setbacks. It's about understanding that true growth happens outside your comfort zone, and that those moments of challenge are actually fertile ground for blossoming into a stronger, more resilient, and more self-aware individual.

For ENFPs, with your sensitivity to criticism and perfectionistic streaks, cultivating a growth mindset is especially important. It's about replacing that fear of failure with a hunger for lessons learned. It's about redefining "mistakes" as stepping stones. Think of yourself as a sculptor, constantly chipping away at the raw material of your life, transforming it into a masterpiece over time.

Here's how to strengthen those growth muscles:

Change Your Narrative: Question the stories you tell yourself. Is "I'm terrible at this" serving you, or is it fueling a self-defeating cycle? Try "I'm learning," or "This is a challenging step, and I'm capable of figuring it out."

Seek Out Spicy Challenges: Too much comfort breeds stagnation. Push yourself to try things slightly beyond your current abilities.

Sign up for that dance class you've been eyeing, attempt a new skill, or put yourself in a situation that requires you to think differently.

Embrace the Power of "Yet": Add this magical word to the end of self-limiting thoughts. "I can't write a book" becomes "I can't write a book...yet". Simple shift, but it keeps the possibility alive.

Focus on the Process: Let go of the obsession with the final product. Relish the journey: the research, the experimentation, the tiny wins along the way. This takes the pressure off and makes learning fun again.

Feedback = Fuel: Actively seek constructive feedback, even when it stings a bit. See it as a treasure map pointing towards areas for improvement rather than an indictment of your worth.

Celebrate Your Past Selves: Acknowledge how far you've come. Compare your current self to where you were a year ago, even a month ago! This provides tangible evidence of your growth and boosts motivation.

This chapter is about equipping yourself with the mindset to take those sometimes scary leaps that lead to expansion and fulfillment. It's about trusting your ability to adapt, to bounce back from setbacks, and to view challenges as opportunities disguised as really annoying inconveniences.

TURNING "SHOULDS" INTO "WANTS": LIVING LIFE ON YOUR OWN TERMS

ENFPs, with your adventurous spirit and deep desire to make your life a meaningful masterpiece, are often susceptible to a dangerous trap: the "shoulds." These are the external expectations, the societal norms, the well-intentioned advice from loved ones, that subtly and not-so-subtly nudge you down a path that feels "safe" or "practical," even if it quietly erodes your soul.

Picture this: You've always dreamed of running your own creative business, but a voice whispers, "You *should* get a stable job with benefits." Or you long to take a solo backpacking trip, yet another voice insists you *should* settle down and start a family. These "shoulds" can create a profound dissonance, leaving you feeling unfulfilled, restless, and wondering if there's something wrong with you for not fitting neatly into the conventional mold.

Why "Shoulds" are So Dangerous for ENFPs

Here's why living a "should" driven life is a recipe for ENFP disaster:

- Authenticity vs. Conformity: ENFPs crave a life aligned with their values, not dictated by what others deem appropriate. "Shoulds" create inner conflict, eroding your sense of self.
- Creativity Killer: Following a prescribed path leaves little room for the innovation, spontaneity, and joy that fuel your spirit. You start coloring inside the lines, dimming your vibrant spark.
- Lost Opportunities: Time is precious. Years spent pursuing someone else's definition of success are years you can't

reclaim following your own dreams. Regret stings more than failure for an ENFP.

- Resentment Builds: Suppressing your passions can breed resentment towards yourself and others, tainting even the "good" parts of your life.

Transforming "Shoulds" into "Wants"

Here's how to break free and design a life truly your own:

1. Identify the Enemy: Become a "should" detective. Notice when your decisions are driven by guilt, obligation, or fear of what others think. Question the origin of these "shoulds" – are they yours, or someone else's?

2. Connect with Your Values: What truly matters to you? What makes your heart sing, regardless of external validation? Write it down, making your inner compass crystal clear.

3. Dissect the Fear: What are you afraid will happen if you defy those "shoulds"? Disappointment from others? Financial insecurity? Challenge these fears with logic and evidence to the contrary.

4. Envision Your "Want" Life: Paint a vivid picture of what living on your terms would feel like. Use this vision as fuel when the "shoulds" get loud.

5. Baby Steps Build Bravery: Start small. Defying a minor "should" boosts confidence for tackling the bigger ones. Order the "weird" dish no one else would, or wear that quirky outfit you love but worry is "too much".

6. The Power of Choice: Remind yourself that even when external circumstances feel constricting, you always have the power to choose your mindset and attitude.

7. Find Your "Rebel" Tribe: Surround yourself with people who champion your dreams and understand your desire to go against the grain. Their support is invaluable!

This chapter is a battle cry for authenticity. It's about giving yourself permission to embrace those offbeat desires and carving out a life that feels expansive, joyous, and unapologetically you.

Remember, fitting in is vastly overrated. The world needs more people living life on their own terms, blazing a trail that inspires others to do the same.

Let the "shoulds" fall away like dead leaves in autumn, making space for the vibrant, messy, and extraordinarily beautiful life that only you can design!

FINDING YOUR VOICE: SPEAKING UP AS AN ENFP

ENFPs have a unique gift for communication. Your words flow with warmth, enthusiasm, and an ability to connect with others on a heart level. You can inspire with your vision, comfort a hurting friend with just the right phrase, and cut through tension with a well-timed joke. But there's a flip side. Sometimes your desire for harmony, your fear of conflict, or simply those whirlwind thoughts getting jammed in your mouth can make it difficult to speak your truth, assert your needs, or have the tough conversations that authentic living requires.

This chapter is about finding your voice in all its multifaceted forms – from those loud, passionate declarations born from deep conviction to the quiet moments of standing firm in your own worth. It's about using your communication superpowers for good, both in your own life, and in the broader world that so desperately needs your voice.

When It's Hard to Speak Up

Let's explore those moments when your ENFP eloquence seems to desert you:

- People-Pleasing Takes Over: Your deep desire to be liked and to create harmony can make you minimize your own needs to avoid rocking the boat.
- Fear of Judgement: Expressing a differing opinion or putting yourself out there risks criticism, and that can trigger deep-seated ENFP insecurities.
- Overthinking Overload: Your mind races through all potential outcomes of speaking up, the "what ifs" paralyzing you into silence.
- Sensitivity + Intensity: You feel things deeply, and those

strong emotions can be overwhelming, especially when it comes to addressing conflict.

Your Voice Matters, ENFP!

Here's why finding your voice is essential:

- Authenticity = Freedom: Speaking your truth, even when it's difficult, is an act of self-love and leads to a more fulfilling life.
- Stronger Connections: Honest communication builds deeper trust and intimacy in your relationships.
- Advocacy Power: Your voice has the potential to make a positive impact, whether it's standing up for yourself, defending a cause, or sharing your unique perspective.
- Ripple Effect: Courage is contagious. Speaking up empowers others around you to do the same.

Unlock Your Voice: The Toolkit

Here's how to find your voice and use it wisely:

1. Practice in Safe Spaces: Start by asserting yourself in low-stakes situations. Disagree politely during a casual debate, or set a small boundary with a friend. Build confidence gradually.
2. Find Your "Why": Connect with your purpose for speaking up. Is it about aligning with your values? Helping a loved one? This fuels your courage when doubt creeps in.
3. Mindfulness Matters: Manage strong emotions that might hijack your message. Take a few breaths, ground yourself, then communicate from a centered place.
4. Assertive vs. Aggressive: There's strength in kindness. You can be direct and set boundaries without sacrificing compassion. "I understand your view, and here's what I need..." is powerful.
5. It Doesn't Have to Be Perfect: Stumbling over words is okay! Authenticity often matters more than eloquent speeches.
6. The Power of Writing: If verbalizing is hard, write it out first.

Scripting a difficult conversation or journaling to organize your thoughts helps clarify your message.

This chapter is a call to action. It's about recognizing the unique power of your words and your right to be heard. It's about facing those fears head-on, finding the courage to speak your truth, and using your voice for positive change, starting with your own beautifully authentic life.

The world, ever noisy and chaotic, needs your ENFP perspective, your compassionate wisdom, and your unwavering belief in a better future. Don't let your voice remain trapped in the land of unspoken possibilities.

THE ENFP MANIFESTO: PERMISSION TO BE YOURSELF

ENFP, this is your battle cry, your love letter, your call to arms. This is where you drop the weight of all those expectations, shed the layers of doubt, and embrace the glorious, scattered, exuberant, and sometimes exhausting journey that is being authentically you.

You've spent long enough dimming your light. Trying to cram your brilliant, multifaceted self into boxes designed for others. This chapter is your permission slip to rip up those blueprints, toss confetti in the face of conformity, and live a life that dances to the beat of your own wonderfully offbeat heart.

Let's dissect what makes you extraordinary, shall we?

- Your Infectious Energy: You enter a room and it's like someone flipped a switch from dull to dazzling. Your enthusiasm fuels others, inspires joy, and makes dreary tasks feel like a delightful adventure.
- The Big-Picture Visionary: Where others see problems, you see potential. Your ability to imagine a better world, a happier workplace, a more fulfilling relationship – that's the stuff that drives positive change.
- Empath Extraordinaire: You feel deeply, both the heart wrenching pain and the exquisite joy. This makes you a fiercely loyal friend, a compassionate advocate, and someone who understands the power of a well-timed hug.
- Master of Connection: Small talk bores your soul. You crave those heart-to-heart conversations that crack people open, reveal their true selves, and forge bonds that transcend the superficial.
- Idea Machine: Your mind is a kaleidoscope, constantly

spitting out brilliant possibilities. Some might call you flighty; we prefer creatively prolific.

Of course, it wouldn't be an honest manifesto without acknowledging some struggles:

- **Self-Doubt Demon:** That pesky voice that questions your brilliance, holds you back from risks, and whispers that you're not smart enough, disciplined enough, fill-in-the-blank enough.
- **FOMO Central:** Fear of missing out drives you to overcommit, sacrificing well-being and sometimes burning bridges when you can't follow through.
- **The Sensitivity Struggle:** Criticism stings, your emotions can overwhelm, and your urge to fix the world's suffering can lead to burnout.
- **Squirrel!:** Oh, the siren song of shiny new possibilities! Staying focused on a single project until completion can sometimes feel like torture.

Embrace Your Weird, Wonderful Self: The Manifesto

1. **Perfection is the Enemy of Awesome:** Strive for progress, not some unattainable, imaginary ideal. Celebrate small wins, laugh at your stumbles, and remember, done is better than perfect!
2. **Nurture Your Joy:** Your enthusiasm is contagious, but also replenishable. Schedule those activities that recharge your soul like they're non-negotiable doctor's appointments.
3. **Feelings Are Your Fuel:** Don't numb them; express them. Find healthy outlets for your joy, anger, and everything in between. Learn to manage emotional intensity, so it doesn't manage you.
4. **Focus: Shiny Things Are Deceptive:** Practice channeling your brilliant curiosity into deep dives on projects, not just flitting between them. The reward of accomplishment is worth the temporary discomfort.
5. **"No" is a Complete Sentence:** Learn to set boundaries without

guilt. Your time, energy, and talents are precious; spend them wisely.

6.   Seek Out Your Squad: Surround yourself with people who get your quirky humor, respect your sensitive side, and champion your dreams, even those that change weekly.

7.   Your Difference is Your Superpower: Stop trying to fit in. Your unique blend of enthusiasm, big ideas, and genuine kindness is exactly what the world craves, so don't hide it!

This chapter is your reminder that being an ENFP isn't a curse, it's a gift. Sure, you'll face challenges. Your wiring is different, and that's okay...it's amazing! Own your quirks, be kind to yourself, and dare to live a life that shines as bright as the beautiful chaos inside your magnificent ENFP mind.

WHEN THE WORLD NEEDS MORE ENFPS: YOUR UNIQUE IMPACT

The world is loud, messy, and often feels like it's teetering on the edge of chaos. In the face of overwhelming problems, cynicism creeps in, hope seems naive, and the temptation to retreat into apathy is real. But this is precisely where ENFPs are needed most. Your idealism, your unquenchable enthusiasm, and your unwavering belief in the potential for good are potent antidotes to the negativity that threatens to drown out the possibility of a better future.

Why ENFPs Are World-Changers in Waiting

Let's explore how your unique superpowers can make a tangible difference:

- Sparking Hope: When others see only darkness, you see opportunity. Your optimism is infectious, reminding people that even small acts of kindness can create ripples that change the world.
- Advocacy with Heart: You don't just talk about injustice, you feel it on a visceral level. This empathy translates into powerful advocacy, fueled by a genuine desire for a world where everyone is valued and has the chance to thrive.
- Connection Catalysts: In a society that's increasingly divided, ENFPs build bridges. You find common ground, bring people together, and facilitate conversations that foster understanding and collaboration.
- Creativity Unleashed: You see the world not just as it is, but as it could be. This fuels innovation in all fields, transforming problems into opportunities, and reminding us that progress needs imagination.
- Championing the Underdogs: Your deep sense of

compassion draws you to uplift voices that are silenced, defend the marginalized, and fight for a world where everyone has a seat at the table.

ENFPs in Action: Areas Ripe for Impact

Where can you channel your passion and talents for the greatest good? Here are just a few possibilities:

- Social Justice: Advocate for causes you believe in, whether it's fighting for equality, protecting the environment, or ensuring equal access to resources. Your voice and passion can inspire others to join the cause.
- Community Building: ENFPs thrive on connection. Create spaces, online or in person, where people feel seen, heard, and empowered to come together for positive change in their local communities.
- Creative Arts: Your ability to inspire and uplift is potent in the arts. Whether it's through writing, music, visual arts, or performance, use your creative voice to spark empathy, challenge perspectives, and offer hope.
- Entrepreneurship with a Twist: Starting a business with a focus on social responsibility or innovative solutions that benefit society is an ENFP's dream come true – you get to use your ideas to make a difference and have flexibility!
- Mentorship: Share your warmth and encouragement by mentoring young people, especially those who feel lost or misunderstood. Your belief in them can unlock their hidden potential.

Amplifying Your Impact

To make the biggest splash, remember:

- Focus Your Fire: While ENFPs are multitalented, channel your energy into a few key areas where you can make a sustained impact, not just scattered, fleeting efforts.
- Collaboration is King: Partner with detail-oriented, practical types who complement your big-picture vision. Together,

you're unstoppable.
- Self-Care is Essential: Empathy burnout is real. Protect your energy so you can keep shining bright for the causes that fuel your soul.

This chapter is a call to action. Don't underestimate the power of your idealism, your kindness, and your bold, beautiful ENFP spirit. The world doesn't just need solutions; it desperately needs people who believe those solutions are possible, who refuse to settle for the status quo, who dare to fight for a brighter future with unyielding optimism and infectious enthusiasm.

THE GIFT OF BEING DIFFERENT: LOVING YOUR ENFP SELF

In a world that often values conformity, productivity, and emotional stoicism, being an ENFP can feel like you're a vibrant, wildly enthusiastic unicorn in a beige corporate office. You might long to fit in, to feel "normal," to quiet that whirlwind in your mind just for a moment. But here's the glorious truth: being different is your greatest strength. This chapter is about embracing those quirky, messy, beautiful aspects of yourself that make you uniquely you.

Understanding Why You Feel Different

Let's dissect why fitting the mold feels so elusive for ENFPs:

- Your Energy is Exuberant: When most people are shuffling along in neutral, you're buzzing with enthusiasm. This can be misinterpreted as restlessness, immaturity, or a lack of seriousness.
- You Think Outside the Box: You see potential where others see limitations. Your unconventional solutions can leave more structured thinkers baffled or threatened.
- Feelings Matter: You wear your heart on your sleeve, while much of the world prefers a mask of stoicism. Your sensitivity might be labeled as being overly dramatic or thin-skinned.
- Idea Fountain: Your mind never stops churning out possibilities. This can lead to unfinished projects and overwhelm those who prefer a clear, linear path.
- Hunger for Connection: Small talk bores you. You crave deep connection, which can feel intrusive or overly intense to those who prefer to keep things surface level.

The Benefits of Being Uniquely You

Embrace your unicorn-ness, ENFP! Here's what those "flaws" actually are:

- Joy Magnet: Your enthusiasm attracts positivity and fuels others, reminding them that life can be fun, not just a series of obligations.
- Creative Powerhouse: Your ability to see unusual connections leads to innovation and helps find solutions others miss completely.
- Empathy Beacon: Your capacity for deep feeling makes you a compassionate friend, an advocate for the overlooked, and a beacon of warmth in a cold world.
- Possibility Explorer: Your constant stream of ideas opens doors others don't even see. You push boundaries and inspire progress.
- Connection Catalyst: Your gift for drawing people in creates strong communities, inspires collaboration, and helps others feel heard and understood.

Self-Love: The ENFP Superpower

Here's how to cultivate that superpower and finally make peace with your wonderfully unique wiring:

- Challenge Negative Self-Talk: That inner critic loves to twist your differences into defects. Replace "I'm too scattered" with "My mind is capable of creative brilliance".
- Befriend Your Emotions: Allow yourself to feel, both the joy and the pain. Develop healthy tools to express, process, and ride those emotional waves without feeling overwhelmed.
- Celebrate Your Strengths: Focus on what your ENFP superpowers allow you to do, not the perceived shortcomings. Keep a "wins" journal to highlight your accomplishments.
- Seek Support: Surround yourself with people who appreciate your quirks and champion your growth. Join ENFP communities where your brand of weird is totally

normal!

- Self-Care as Rebellion: In a world that pressures constant productivity, prioritize rest, play, and activities that replenish your soul.

This chapter is a love letter to your messy, quirky, enthusiastic ENFP self. The world needs your unique brand of sparkle – your big ideas, your warm heart, and your unwavering belief in the potential for good. Stop trying to dim your light to fit in. Instead, focus on channeling your energy, managing those ENFP-specific challenges, and embracing the beautiful, unique, and world-changing individual that you are.

YOUR IDEA FACTORY IS WIDE OPEN: THE JOURNEY CONTINUES...

ENFP, think of your journey of self-discovery as a magnificent, ever-evolving amusement park. You've explored the thrilling rollercoasters of your emotions, navigated the dizzying house of mirrors that is your ever-changing mind, savored the sweetness of connecting with kindred spirits, and conquered some of those pesky demons like perfectionism and self-doubt.

But here's the glorious thing: This amusement park never closes. The joy of being an ENFP lies in the endless possibilities for growth, self-discovery, and making a positive impact on your little corner of the world...and beyond!

What's Next on Your Adventure?

While no one can map out your exact path, here are some exciting possibilities to consider:

- Deep Dives: You've learned the fundamentals of your ENFP superpowers and pitfalls. Now, choose an area that sparks your curiosity and dive deeper. Maybe it's developing your emotional intelligence, mastering project completion, or refining your communication skills.
- Experimentation Station: This is your life, and it's the ultimate creative playground! Try new things that scare and excite you. Learn a skill you've always admired, take a solo trip, put yourself out there in ways that stretch your comfort zone. Growth lies just outside its borders.
- Contribution Exploration: You want to make a difference, now how? Volunteer for a cause you care about, use your creative skills for the greater good, or simply look for ways to

spread kindness and joy in your everyday life.

- Mindfulness Matters: Your introspective nature can be a strength. Integrate mindfulness practices into your routine to calm your busy mind, manage intensity, and deepen your self-awareness.
- Community is Key: Keep building those connections with like-minded souls. Attend workshops or retreats tailored to ENFPs, or join online communities. Share your journey, learn from others, and form supportive, inspiring bonds.

The Ongoing Quest: Self-Compassion

The path won't always be smooth. You'll have days of doubt, procrastination battles, and moments of feeling overwhelmed by your own intensity. That's where self-compassion is key. Here's how to cultivate it:

- Talk to yourself kindly: Notice your inner critic and replace harsh words with understanding. "This is hard AND I can learn" beats "I'm such a mess" any day.
- Celebrate Small Wins: Progress isn't always linear. Recognize the baby steps, the lessons learned from the stumbles, and the courage it takes to keep showing up.
- It's a Journey, Not a Destination: Release the pressure to be a "perfect" ENFP. Growth is a lifelong process, full of zigs, zags, and occasional rides you regret but have hilarious stories from later.

Remember, You're Not Alone

This book has been your companion, but your journey is far from over. Here are resources to support you along the way:

- ENFP Communities: Find them online or in your local area. Connecting with people who "get" you is incredibly validating and offers support on your unique path.
- Therapy Tailored to ENFPs: A skilled therapist who understands your personality type can help you navigate challenges, develop coping mechanisms, and celebrate your

wins.

- Books & Articles: Seek out resources specifically for ENFPs. They offer valuable insights, strategies, and reminders that you're not broken, just differently wired.

Dear ENFP, this is your send-off, your gentle nudge out into the world. Go forth, armed with a deeper understanding of yourself, a newfound appreciation for your quirks, and a toolkit for thriving in a world that doesn't always understand your dazzling brand of magic. Remember, your enthusiasm, your big heart, and your unwavering belief in a better world are the gifts you're meant to share.

www.ingramcontent.com/pod-product-compliance
Lightning Source LLC
Chambersburg PA
CBHW051655250726
48653CB00007B/2678